Isaac Newton

and Gravity

Yoming S. Lin

PowerKiDS
press

New York

To Ivy, you are like an older sister to me. You are my gravity—you are always there for me, keeping me grounded. Thank you, with love.

Published in 2012 by The Rosen Publishing Group, Inc.
29 East 21st Street, New York, NY 10010

First Edition

Editor: Amelie von Zumbusch
Book Design: Greg Tucker

Photo Credits: Cover (Isaac Newton), p. 20 (top left) Anonymous/The Bridgeman Art Library/ Getty Images; cover (apple), pp. 5, 6, 9 (top, bottom), 10, 11, 13 (top, bottom), 17 (top), 20 (bottom) Shutterstock.com; pp. 4, 21 (top) Sir Godfrey Kneller/Getty Images; p. 7 Time Life Pictures/Mansell/ Getty Images; p. 8 Louis-Francois Roubillac/The Bridgeman Art Library/Getty Images; pp. 12, 16 Photos.com/Thinkstock; pp. 14, 19 Hemera/Thinkstock; pp. 15, 17 (bottom), 20 (top right) Science & Society Picture Library/Getty Images; p. 18 Sir James Thornhill/Getty Images; p. 21 (bottom) Bob Thomas/Popperfoto/Getty Images.

Library of Congress Cataloging-in-Publication Data

Lin, Yoming S.
  Isaac Newton and gravity / by Yoming S. Lin. — 1st ed.
     p. cm. — (Eureka!)
  Includes index.
  ISBN 978-1-4488-5032-7 (library binding)
  1. Newton, Isaac, Sir, 1642-1727—Juvenile literature. 2. Physicists—Great Britain—Biography— Juvenile literature. 3. Gravity—Juvenile literature. I. Title. II. Series.
  QC16.N7L56 2012
  530.092—dc22
  [B]

2011001724

Manufactured in the United States of America

CPSIA Compliance Information: Batch #WS11PK: For Further Information contact Rosen Publishing, New York, New York at 1-800-237-9932

Contents

A Great Scientist 4

Early Life 6

The College Student 8

Gravity 10

His Famous Work 12

Light and Colors 14

Great Success 16

Changing Science 18

Timeline 20

Inside the Science 22

Glossary 23

Index 24

Web Sites 24

A Great Scientist

Why does an apple fall from a tree? When you jump up, why do you always fall back down? The scientist Isaac Newton figured out that these things happen because of a force called gravity that pulls objects toward Earth. Newton used math to show that gravity also makes the Moon travel around Earth. Other scientists had not been able to

Isaac Newton was a very smart scientist. However, he often had trouble getting along with people.

Gravity is what pulls you back to Earth after you jump up while jumping rope. It also pulls the rope down after you swing it up.

figure out how the Moon does this. Newton came up with laws to describe how objects move, too.

Along with making great discoveries, Newton changed how scientists work. He helped shape the **scientific method**. This is the method scientists use to answer scientific questions.

Isaac Newton was born on December 25, 1642, in Woolsthorpe, England. His mother was named Hannah and his father was named Isaac. The older Isaac died before his son was born. When young Isaac was three years old, his mother married again. After this, his

Isaac Newton was born in this house, called Woolsthorpe Manor. It is in the village of Woolsthorpe. The village is also known by its longer name, Woolsthorpe by Colsterworth.

The English Civil War lasted through most of Isaac Newton's childhood. It was fought between English people who backed kings and those who did not.

grandmother took care of him. He did not spend much time with his mother.

In 1653, Isaac Newton's stepfather died. His mother returned to Woolsthorpe. At this time, he was taken out of school so he could take care of the family farm. He did not like farming and was not a good farmer. After a short time, he went back to school.

Newton entered the University of Cambridge in Cambridge, England, in 1661. There, he became interested in science and math. Newton **graduated**, or finished his studies, in 1665. He hoped to stay on at Cambridge to study more. Later that year,

Cambridge is made up of many colleges. Newton studied at Trinity College. Trinity's chapel is now home to this statue of Newton.

though, Cambridge closed down because of an outbreak of a sickness called the **plague**.

Newton went home for several years. There, he thought about lights and color. He studied how objects move in the sky, too. He also worked on a new type of advanced math, called **calculus**. Newton later remembered seeing an apple fall from a tree during this time. He said that this was what got him started thinking about gravity.

Top: This is one of the courtyards at Trinity College, Cambridge.
Bottom: To this day, the name Isaac Newton makes many people think of apple trees!

Gravity

Newton returned to Cambridge in 1667. In 1679, scientist Robert Hooke wrote to Newton. Both men wanted to explain the movements of objects in space. Hooke thought that a force pulled all objects toward each other but could not prove it. Newton used math to show how objects are pulled toward other objects by gravity.

People, such as this astronaut, float when they go up into space. This is because they are too far from Earth for its gravity to hold them in place.

Earth's gravity makes sports like skateboarding possible. Without gravity, you would just keep rising up into the sky when you jumped.

Gravity acts on objects because they have **mass**. Mass is the amount of **matter** an object has. The more mass an object has, the stronger its gravitational pull will be. Gravity pulls an apple toward Earth and also pulls Earth toward the apple. Earth is huge compared to the apple, so its pull is much stronger. The apple falls to the ground while Earth stays still.

His Famous Work

Gravity also explains the movements of objects in space. Earth's gravity pulls the Moon toward it. This keeps the Moon in its **orbit**, or path, around Earth. Gravity also holds the planets in their orbits around the Sun. Newton described his law of gravity in his book the *Principia*.

This is the first page of the *Principia*. The book's longer name, *Philosophiae Naturalis Principia Mathematica*, means "Mathematical Principles of Natural Philosophy," in Latin.

PHILOSOPHIÆ
NATURALIS
PRINCIPIA
MATHEMATICA.

Autore JS. NEWTON, Trin. Coll. Cantab. Soc. Matheseos
Professore Lucasiano, & Societatis Regalis Sodali.

IMPRIMATUR.
S. PEPYS, Reg. Soc. PRÆSES.
Julii 5. 1686.

R. ASTRON. SOC.

LONDINI,
Jussu Societatis Regiæ ac Typis Josephi Streater. Prostat apud
plures Bibliopolas. Anno MDCLXXXVII.

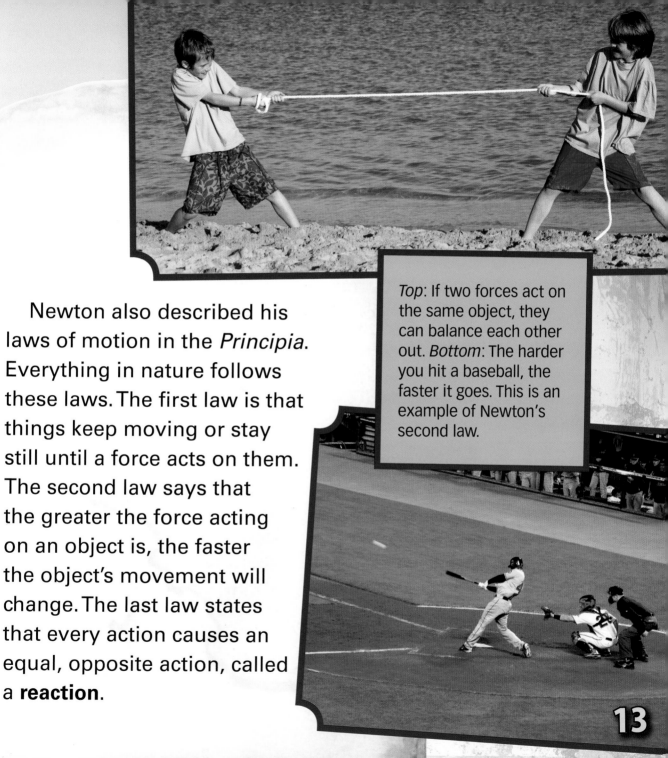

Newton also described his laws of motion in the *Principia*. Everything in nature follows these laws. The first law is that things keep moving or stay still until a force acts on them. The second law says that the greater the force acting on an object is, the faster the object's movement will change. The last law states that every action causes an equal, opposite action, called a **reaction**.

Top: If two forces act on the same object, they can balance each other out. *Bottom*: The harder you hit a baseball, the faster it goes. This is an example of Newton's second law.

Light and Colors

In 1704, Newton's book on lights and colors, *Opticks*, came out. Through experiments, Newton had seen that white sunlight is made up of all the colors in the rainbow. He let sunlight pass through a glass object called a **prism**. The light separated into different colors. Newton used another prism to show that these colors could not be separated further. However, the different color lights could be combined together to become white light again.

This prism has split a ray of white light to form the rainbow on the wall behind it. Prisms most often have three sides.

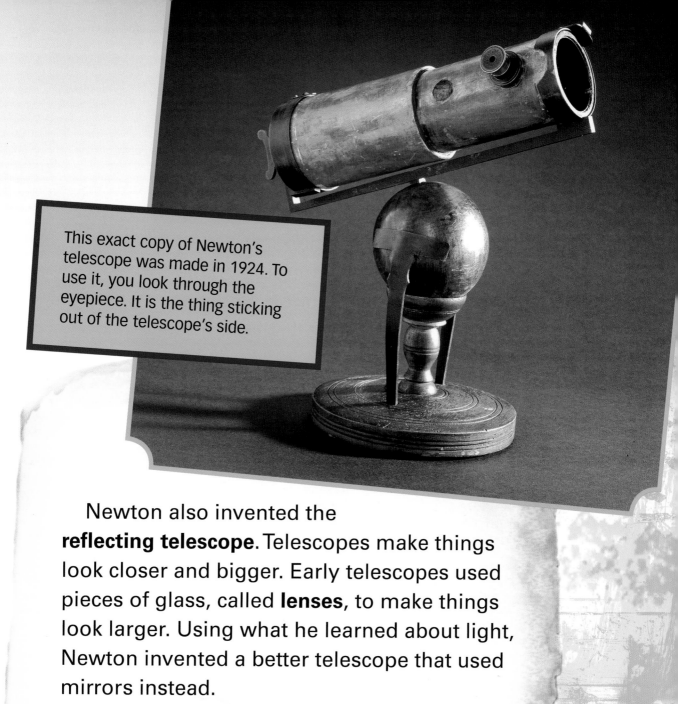

This exact copy of Newton's telescope was made in 1924. To use it, you look through the eyepiece. It is the thing sticking out of the telescope's side.

Newton also invented the **reflecting telescope**. Telescopes make things look closer and bigger. Early telescopes used pieces of glass, called **lenses**, to make things look larger. Using what he learned about light, Newton invented a better telescope that used mirrors instead.

Great Success

After Newton invented his telescope, he was picked to be a member of the Royal Society. This was a group of important English scientists.

In 1696, Newton started working for the Royal **Mint** in London, England. The mint is where money

In his later years, Newton moved to London. He lived in this house on St. Martin's Street in a part of London called Westminster from 1710 until 1725.

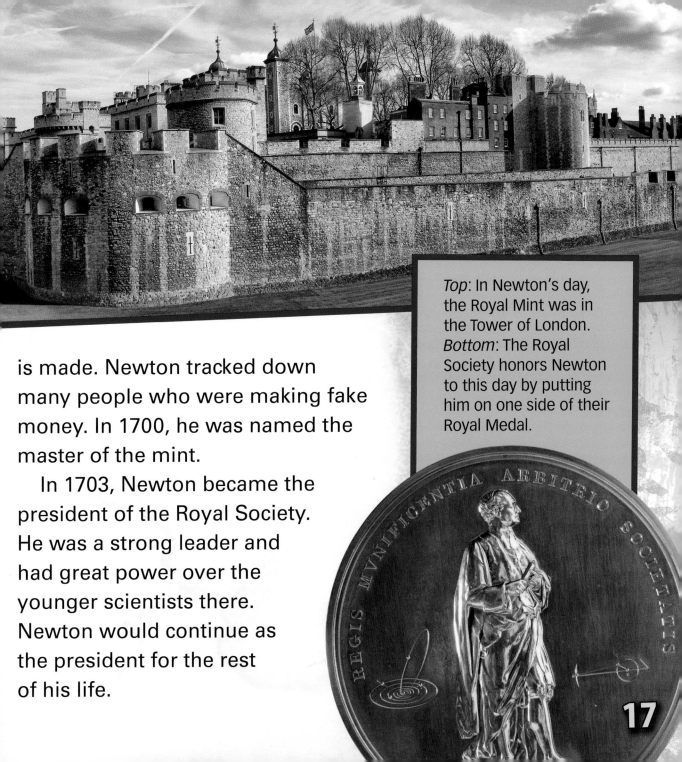

Top: In Newton's day, the Royal Mint was in the Tower of London. *Bottom*: The Royal Society honors Newton to this day by putting him on one side of their Royal Medal.

is made. Newton tracked down many people who were making fake money. In 1700, he was named the master of the mint.

In 1703, Newton became the president of the Royal Society. He was a strong leader and had great power over the younger scientists there. Newton would continue as the president for the rest of his life.

17

Changing Science

In 1705, England's Queen Anne made Newton a knight. He was the first scientist to get this honor for his work. After being knighted, he was known as Sir Isaac Newton.

Newton died in 1727. Today, he is considered the father of modern **physics**. Physics is the study of energy, or how much work something can do, and matter, or what things are made of.

In his later years, Newton was honored as one of the greatest scientists of his time. He exchanged letters with scientists from across Europe.

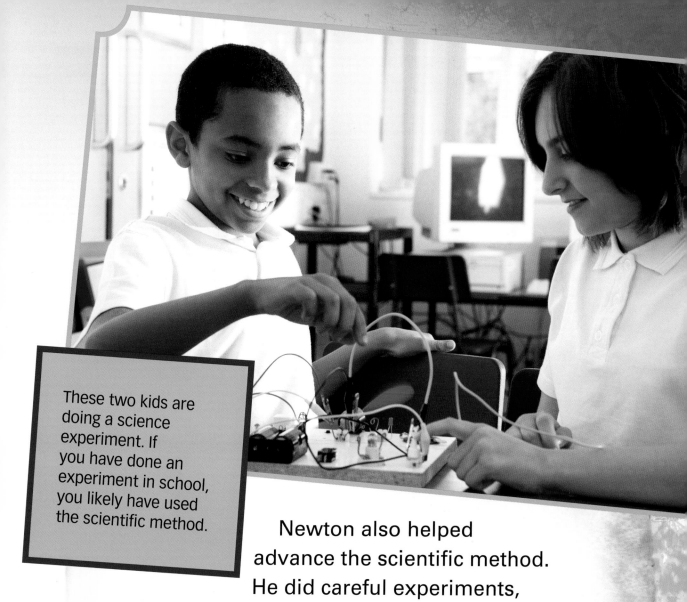

These two kids are doing a science experiment. If you have done an experiment in school, you likely have used the scientific method.

Newton also helped advance the scientific method. He did careful experiments, measured things, and studied results. He wrote down his steps so other scientists could repeat the experiments. Today, scientists still use his methods.

Timeline

England did not switch to the calendar we use today until 1752. The dates here are from the older Julian calendar.

January 11, 1672

Newton is elected to the Royal Society after presenting his reflecting telescope.

August 1653

Newton's mother moves back to Woolsthorpe with her three children from her second marriage.

August 22, 1642

The English Civil War breaks out between followers of King Charles I and backers of Parliament.

1630   1640   1650   1660   1670   1680

June 5, 1661

Newton starts classes at the University of Cambridge's Trinity College.

December 25, 1642

Isaac Newton is born in Woolsthorpe, England.

August 1684

The scientist Edmond Halley visits Newton to talk about the movement of the planets.

February 1700

Newton becomes the master of the mint in London, England.

July 5, 1687

Newton's book the *Principia* comes out.

November 30, 1703

Newton becomes the president of the Royal Society.

1690 1700 1710 1720 1730 1740

March 20, 1727

Newton dies in London. He is buried in Westminster Abbey, the most famous church in England.

February 13, 1689

William and Mary are crowned the king and queen of England several months after James II is driven from the throne.

21

Inside the Science

1. The closer objects are to each other, the stronger their gravitational pull is. The closer something is to Earth, the harder Earth pulls on it. People who go into space float because they are too far from Earth to be pulled down by its gravity.

2. Newton's first law of motion says that things keep moving or stay still until a force acts upon them. If you throw a ball up into the air, gravity is the force that pulls it down.

3. If you give something a push, it will stop moving at some point even if it does not seem to hit anything else. This is because a force called **friction** acts between the object and the surface on which it is moving. Friction slows the object down.

4. Newton's second law of motion says that the greater the force acting on something is, the faster the change will be. If you do not pedal very hard on a bicycle, the bicycle will start moving slowly. If you pedal harder, though, you will start moving faster more quickly.

5. Newton's third law of motion states that for every action, there is an equal and opposite reaction. If you throw a ball hard, you will find yourself falling backward.

Glossary

calculus (KAL-kyuh-lus) An advanced kind of math.

friction (FRIK-shin) The rubbing of one thing against another.

graduated (GRA-jeh-wayt-ed) To have finished a course of school.

lenses (LENZ-ez) Clear, curved parts of the eye or pieces of glass that focus light.

mass (MAS) The amount of matter in something.

matter (MA-ter) Anything that has weight and takes up space.

mint (MINT) A place where a country's money is made.

orbit (OR-bit) A circular path.

physics (FIH-ziks) The scientific study of matter and energy and their relationships to each other.

plague (PLAYG) A very bad illness.

prism (PRIH-zum) A block of glass that separates white light into the colors of the rainbow.

reaction (ree-AK-shun) An action caused by something that has happened.

reflecting telescope (rih-FLEKT-ing TEH-leh-skohp) A tool that uses mirrors to make faraway things appear bigger and closer.

scientific method (sy-en-TIH-fik MEH-thud) The system of running experiments in science.

Index

A
apple, 4, 9, 11

C
calculus, 9

D
discoveries, 5

E
Earth, 4, 11–12, 22

F
force, 4, 10, 13, 22
friction, 22

L
law(s), 5, 12–13, 22
lenses, 15

M
mass, 11
math, 4, 8–10
Moon, 4–5, 12

O
orbit(s), 12

P
physics, 18
prism, 14

Q
questions, 5

R
reaction, 13, 22
reflecting telescope,
    15, 20
Royal Mint, 16

S
scientific method, 5, 19

W
Woolsthorpe, England,
    6–7, 20

Web Sites

Due to the changing nature of Internet links, PowerKids Press has developed an online list of Web sites related to the subject of this book. This site is updated regularly. Please use this link to access the list:
www.powerkidslinks.com/eure/newton/